the SCIENCE beHIND

TRICKS OF SOUND AND LIGHT

Nicolas Brasch

- ➥ Why Can Dogs Hear Sounds That Humans Cannot Hear?

- ➥ Are Black and White Colors?

- ➥ Why Do Objects in Water Look Closer than They Really Are?

A⁺

Smart Apple Media
P.O. Box 3263
Mankato, MN, 56002

First published in 2010 by
MACMILLAN EDUCATION AUSTRALIA PTY LTD
15–19 Claremont St, South Yarra, Australia 3141

Visit our web site at www.macmillan.com.au or go directly to www.macmillanlibrary.com.au

Associated companies and representatives throughout the world.

Copyright © Nicolas Brasch 2010

Library of Congress Cataloging-in-Publication Data

Brasch, Nicolas.
  Tricks of sound and light / Nicolas Brasch.
       p. cm. — (The science behind)
  Includes index.
  ISBN 978-1-59920-564-9 (lib. bdg.)
  1. Sound—Juvenile literature. 2. Light—Juvenile literature. I. Title.
  QC225.5.B729 2011
535—dc22

                                        2009045110

Publisher: Carmel Heron
Managing Editor: Vanessa Lanaway
Editor: Georgina Garner
Proofreader: Kylie Cockle
Designer: Stella Vassiliou
Page layout: Stella Vassiliou and Raul Diche
Photo researcher: Sarah Johnson
Illustrators: Alan Laver, pp. 7 (bottom), 8, 9, 11, 12, 14, 23, 30, 31 (top); Richard Morden, pp. 7 (top), 11, 15, 18, 19, 20, 21, 23 (bottom), 24, 25, 27, 31 (bottom); Melissa Webb, 16; Karen Young, p. 1 and Try This! logo.
Production Controller: Vanessa Johnson

Manufactured in China by Macmillan Production (Asia) Ltd.
Kwun Tong, Kowloon, Hong Kong
Supplier Code: CP December 2009

Acknowledgments

The author and the publisher are grateful to the following for permission to reproduce copyright material:

Front cover photographs:
Firework Display, John Churchman/Getty Images; Prism rainbow, © Stijn Peeters/Shutterstock; Aurora Borealis, © Roman Krochuk/Shutterstock.

Photos courtesy of:
© Bettmann/Corbis, 6; © Steve Kaufman/Corbis, 18 (left); AFP/Getty Images, 28; Gerard Brown/Getty Images, 26; Paul Chesley/Getty Images, 25 (top); Mitch York/Getty Images, 22; © Dennis Guyitt/iStockphoto, 5; © Sven Klaschik/iStockphoto, 4; © Chad Thomas/iStockphoto, 29 (jet); © Duncan Walker/iStockphoto, 13 (top); Commander John Bortniak, NOAA Corps (ret.), 17 (left); Stockxpert, 29 (two people); © arway/Shutterstock, 29 (train); © Willyam Bradberry/Shutterstock, 29 (top); © Lars Christensen/Shutterstock, 29 (street); © Elena Elisseeva/Shutterstock, 14 (bottom left); © Jennifer Griner/Shutterstock, 29 (leaves); © Igor Grochev/Shutterstock, 29 (watch); © Roman Krochuk/Shutterstock, 17 (right); © Darko Novakovic/Shutterstock, 29 (concert, classroom); © Stijn Peeters/Shutterstock, 13 (bottom); © Gary Potts/Shutterstock, 12 (bottom); © Matt Trommer/Shutterstock, 14 (bottom right).

Data from www.lsu.edu/deafness/HearingRange.html, 26.

While every care has been taken to trace and acknowledge copyright, the publisher tenders their apologies for any accidental infringement where copyright has proved untraceable. Where the attempt has been unsuccessful, the publisher welcomes information that would redress the situation.

The publisher would like to thank Heidi Ruhnau, Head of Science at Oxley College, for her assistance in reviewing manuscripts.

Please note
At the time of printing, the Internet addresses appearing in this book were correct. Owing to the dynamic nature of the Internet, however, we cannot guarantee that all these addresses will remain correct.

▶ Contents

Look out for these features throughout the book:

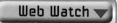

"Word Watch" explains the meanings of words shown in **bold**

"Web Watch" provides web site suggestions for further research

Understanding the World Through Science

Science = Knowledge
The word "science" comes from the Latin word *scientia*, which means "knowledge."

▲ Humans look at the things around them and ask "Why?" and "How?" Science helps answer these questions.

Science is amazing! Through science, people can understand more about the world and themselves. Without science, humans would not have a clue—about anything!

Shared Knowledge

Science exists because humans are curious. They are curious about how things work, about Earth and its place in the universe, about life and survival, about the natural world around them, and about time, space, and speed. They are curious about everything! They never stop asking questions.

Science is the knowledge that humans have gathered about the physical and natural world and how it works. This knowledge is gathered through **experimentation** and **observation**.

Word Watch

experimentation using scientific procedures to make discoveries, test ideas, and prove facts

observation watching carefully in order to gain information

The Science Behind Tricks of Sound and Light

What we hear and what we see do not always seem to make sense. Sound and light can play tricks on us, such as making objects in water look closer than they are. We can create our own tricks with sound and light, too, using devices such as hearing aids and periscopes.

Puzzling Messages

Sight and hearing are the two senses that humans use above all others to survive. These senses decode messages of light and sound and pass these messages to our brains. Sometimes, however, these messages are puzzling.

Scientists have worked out how sound and light move, what their properties are, and whether they can change form. Puzzling **phenomena,** such as rainbows and echoes, can now be explained by science.

▶ A fireworks display uses tricks of sound and light. It is a good example of physics at work.

Why Do I See Fireworks Explode Before I Hear the Explosion?

Light and sound travel at different speeds. Light travels much faster than sound. Over long distances, we see something before we hear it.

Light and Sound Moving at Different Speeds

The speed of light is about 985,000,000 feet (300,000,000 meters) per second, while the speed of sound is about 1125 feet (343 m) per second. This difference in speed is most noticeable over long distances. When watching a fireworks display in the distance, you see fireworks explode before you hear the sound of them exploding. The light reaches your eyes much faster than the sound reaches your ears.

Another example of observing light and sound moving at different speeds is during a lightning storm. Although a flash of lightning and a clap of thunder happen at the same time, you see the lightning before you hear the thunder. The closer you are to the center of the storm, the sooner you will hear the thunder after you have seen the lightning. The light and sound have less distance to travel so the difference in timing is less, too.

Breaking the Sound Barrier

On October 14, 1947, an American pilot, Chuck Yeager (1923–), flew a Bell X-1 airplane to a speed of 670 miles (1078 kilometers) per hour. This is just faster than the speed of sound. Yeager was the first to break what is called the sound barrier.

Scientists had wondered what would happen to a plane that flew faster than sound. Some feared that the plane would not be able to cope and it would break up mid-flight. Yeager's flight showed scientists that when a plane flies faster than the speed of sound, it causes a booming sound. This is called a sonic boom.

▶ Chuck Yeager broke the sound barrier in a Bell X-1 airplane.

Guy Fawkes Night

Guy Fawkes (1570–1606) was a member of a group who planned to blow up the British Houses of Parliament on November 5, 1605. The group planted barrels of gunpowder under Parliament, but their plot was uncovered. Every November 5 is celebrated as Guy Fawkes Night in Britain. Fireworks are set off, representing the gunpowder, and the capture of the group is celebrated.

Test the Speed of Light and Sound

Follow this simple experiment to observe the difference between the speeds of light and sound.

1. Blow up a balloon.

2. Get a friend to hold the balloon and stand at least 115 feet (35 m) away from you.

3. Get your friend to pop the balloon with the pin.

4. Observe what you see and hear. You should see the balloon pop about one-tenth of a second before you hear the pop.

1

115 feet

2

3

sound waves

light waves

4

Faster than Light

No human has ever traveled faster than the speed of light. According to the **theories** of the scientist Albert Einstein (1879–1955), an object would need **infinite** energy for it to travel as fast as light.

▼ When a plane flies faster than the speed of sound, the sound waves it sends out overlap and air pressure builds up. The release of this pressure causes a sonic boom.

sound waves

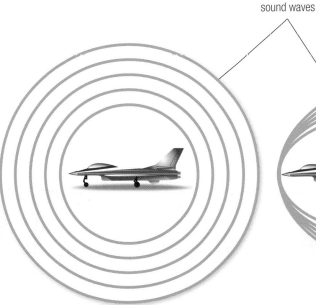

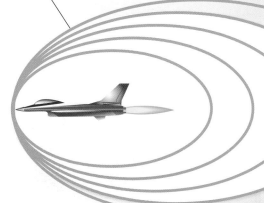

When the plane stands still, sound waves move away from it at 1125 feet (343 m) per second.

As the plane moves faster, the sound waves are compressed.

Word Watch

theories ideas used to explain things

infinite endless and without limit

Web Watch ▼

www.grc.nasa.gov/WWW/K-12/airplane/sound2.html

upload.wikimedia.org/wikipedia/commons/1/1d/SonicBoom.jpg

www.youtube.com/watch?v=uQ2pkmISOLM

How Do Sound and Light Travel Through the Air?

In space, no one can hear you scream—but they can see you scream. This is because sound cannot travel in a **vacuum**, but light can. Sound and light both travel in waves, but they are different types of waves. Sound needs a medium, such as air, to travel through, while light does not.

Measuring Waves

Sound and light waves are both measured by their wavelengths and **frequency**. The bottom of a wave is called a trough. The top of a wave is called a crest.

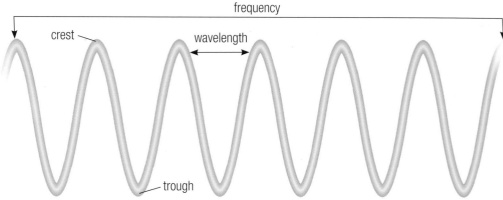

▲ The length of a wave is measured from one crest to the next crest or from one trough to the next trough. The frequency is the number of crests or troughs that pass a particular point over a period of time.

Light Waves

Light is a form of energy that travels in waves. The length of a light wave depends on its color. Each color is a different length. Red light waves are the longest. About 1300 red light waves are packed into just four-hundredths of an inch (1 millimeter). Violet light waves are the shortest. About 600 violet light waves are packed into four-hundredths of an inch (1 mm).

The speed of light, which is almost 186,500 miles (300,000 km) per second, assumes that light waves are traveling through a vacuum. Light waves slow down to different speeds, depending on the substances it passes through.

Word Watch

frequency number of times something occurs in a given time period

vacuum space containing nothing, not even air

Substance	Speed of Light: Miles (KM) Per Second
Vacuum or air	186,200 (299,700)
Water	140,000 (225,000)
Glass	121,200 (195,000)
Diamond	77,700 (125,000)

Sound Waves

Sounds are vibrations that travel in waves. The frequency of sound waves is determined by the number of vibrations that pass a point each second. This frequency is measured in units called hertz (Hz). Long sound waves have low frequencies and produce low sounds. Short sound waves have high frequencies and produce high sounds.

Electromagnetic Spectrum

The electromagnetic spectrum is made up of all types of electromagnetic rays and waves. These rays and waves can travel through vacuums and through other substances such as air. Light is a combination of electrical energy and magnetic energy, so light waves are part of the electromagnetic spectrum.

Sound is not an electromagnetic wave, but it can be carried on radio waves. Sound waves cannot move through a vacuum. They can only move through substances such as air and water.

Hertz

Heinrich Hertz (1857–1894) was a German scientist who conducted an experiment to prove the existence of electromagnetic waves. The unit of measurement for the frequency of waves is called the hertz.

▼ The electromagnetic spectrum is arranged by wavelength, from longest to shortest.

wavelength

wavelength

radio waves

microwaves

infrared light rays

visible light rays

ultraviolet light rays

X rays

gamma rays

The longest waves are radio waves, which can be up to hundreds of feet long.

Light rays are in the middle of the spectrum. Thousands of light rays can be packed into one-tenth of an inch (2.5 mm).

The shortest rays are gamma rays, which have billions of rays packed into one-tenth of an inch (2.5 mm).

Web Watch ▼

imagine.gsfc.nasa.gov/docs/science/know_l1/emspectrum.html

Are Black and White Colors?

Black and white are not colors! When talking about light, white is a combination of all colors mixed together and black is the absence of light. When talking about **pigments**, white is the absence of color and black is a combination of colors.

The Colors of Light

The light around us comes from the sun and from lightbulbs. This light is called white light. When a beam of white light is bent at a particular angle, it breaks into a **spectrum** of colors (see page 13).

Primary Colors of Light

If some colors of light are combined, they will create white light. These colors are red, blue, and green. They are known as the primary colors of light.

▲ When white light is separated out, it produces all the colors of the rainbow.

The Colors of Pigments

Pigments in objects **reflect** only some parts of white light. A red pigment, such as in red paint, **absorbs** all parts of white light except for the red part, which it reflects. When all parts of the light are absorbed by an object, the object appears black.

Creating Color
The colors we see on television or on a computer screen are combinations of colored light. The colors used in paintings and fabrics are combinations of pigments.

Word Watch

absorbs soaks up and reduces the effect of

pigments substances used as coloring

reflect return or bounce back

spectrum band of colors, such as a rainbow, produced by bending light

Primary Colors of Pigments

Yellow, red, and blue are the pigment primary colors. Artists can create the colors they want by mixing yellow, red, and blue in various combinations and quantities.

▶ The primary pigment colors are yellow, red, and blue. Other colors can be made by mixing the primary colors.

Mixing blue and yellow together creates green.

Mixing all three primary colors creates black.

Mixing yellow and red together creates orange.

Mixing red and blue together creates purple.

Try This!

Create White Light

Follow this simple experiment to see how the three primary colors of light make white light.

Materials

- 3 cardboard tubes
- 3 colored **filters** (green, red, and blue)
- Adhesive tape
- 3 torches
- 2 friends

Steps

1. Tape one filter to the end of each tube.

2. Move to a dark room. Each person should hold his or her tube with the filter end pointing toward the floor.

3. Each person should shine a torch through the top of his or her tube.

Observation

The point on the floor where the three colors meet will be white.

Word Watch

filters things that give a light a particular color when light is shone through it

Web Watch ▼

www.colormatters.com/vis_bk_white.html

11

What Is a Rainbow?

Don't try to find the end of a rainbow—you can't. A rainbow is simply an **optical illusion** that sometimes occurs when sunlight passes through raindrops.

Sunlight and Rain

Sunlight and rain must be present for a rainbow to appear in the sky, but the presence of both of these things does not guarantee a rainbow will appear. The sun has to be shining from behind the person viewing the rainbow and the rain has to be falling in front of them.

Colors of the rainbow

When white light is bent, such as when it passes through raindrops or a **prism**, the human eye sees seven colors: red, orange, yellow, green, blue, indigo, and violet. These are known as the colors of the rainbow.

▶ A rainbow is an optical illusion caused by sunlight and rain.

▼ When light passes through a raindrop, it is forced to bend. Red light bends the least and violet light bends the most. In this picture, only the person on the left can see the rainbow.

Word Watch

optical illusion something that the eye sees but is not real

prism triangular-shaped block of glass

Newton's Discovery about White Light

Isaac Newton (1642–1727) made many incredible discoveries. Some of them involved light and color. Newton decided to shine a light onto a prism and see what happened. He showed that white light is made up of different colors. Before Newton's discovery, it was thought that colors were created by adding things to white, not by splitting white light.

▶ Isaac Newton was one of the greatest scientists the world has known.

▼ When light hits a prism, it emerges on the other side in a thick band of separate colors, much like a rainbow.

Try This!

Try Newton's experiment yourself. All you need is a torch and a glass prism.

Shine the torch onto the prism and watch the colored light come out the other side.

A Full Circle

Although a rainbow seems to be an **arc**, it is really part of a circle. The full circle cannot be seen from land, but it can sometimes be seen from an airplane.

Word Watch

arc a semi-circle or curved shape

Web Watch ▼

www.gelighting.com/na/
home_lighting/gela/
students/science_prism.htm

How Are Shadows Formed?

Three things are needed to form a shadow: a light source, an object, and a background to capture the shadow.

Forming a Shadow

Light waves travel in straight lines. When light hits an object that it cannot pass through, a shadow is formed behind the object. The shadow is the area that remains unlit.

Shadow of an Eclipse
Eclipses are caused by shadows. Eclipses occur when a planet, moon, or other **celestial** object moves into the shadow of another object or when it casts a shadow over another object.

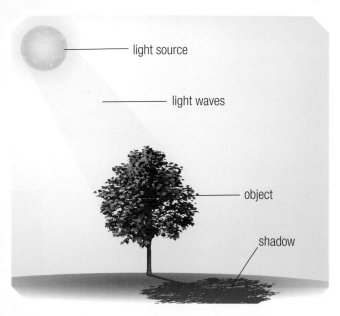

▲ The sun shines on a tree. The background area that is blocked by the tree is in shadow.

▲ Trees are opaque objects, so they cast shadows.

Transparent, Translucent, and Opaque Objects

The type of object that a light shines on is very important. Light can pass through transparent objects, so they form no shadow at all. A plain glass window is an example of a transparent object.

Translucent objects allow some but not all light to pass through them. The light that does pass through is scattered onto the background, leaving a shadow that does not represent the shape of the object.

Opaque objects are solid objects through which light cannot pass. They allow clear shadows to be formed.

◀ Stained-glass windows are translucent, so some light passes through them.

Word Watch

celestial related to the sky or space

Length and Direction of a Shadow

The length and direction of a shadow change according to the position of the light source. In the case of shadows formed by sunlight, the higher the sun is in the sky, the shorter the shadow will be. As the position of the sun in the sky moves throughout the day, so will the position of the shadow.

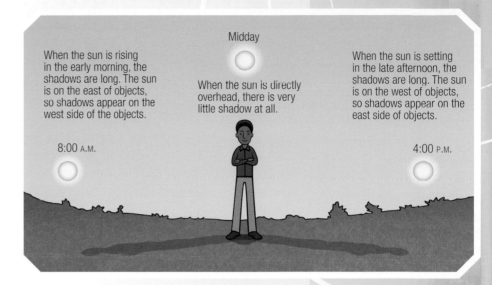

Midday

When the sun is rising in the early morning, the shadows are long. The sun is on the east of objects, so shadows appear on the west side of the objects.

8:00 A.M.

When the sun is directly overhead, there is very little shadow at all.

When the sun is setting in the late afternoon, the shadows are long. The sun is on the west of objects, so shadows appear on the east side of objects.

4:00 P.M.

▲ As the sun moves across the sky, objects cast different kinds of shadows.

The Size of a Shadow

The size of a shadow depends on the distance between the object and the light source. If an object is moved closer to the light source, the shadow gets bigger. If an object is moved away from the light source, the shadow gets smaller.

Try This!

Change the Size of a Shadow

Follow this simple experiment to see how the size of a shadow can change. All you need is a flashlight and a white wall.

1. Hold your hand halfway between the flashlight and the wall. Turn the flashlight on.

2. Move your hand toward the flashlight. Observe how the size of the shadow increases.

3. Move your hand toward the wall. Observe how the size of the shadow decreases.

Web Watch ▼

www.bbc.co.uk/schools/
ks2bitesize/science/
revision_bites/light_
shadows.shtml

What Is a Polar Night?

Polar nights are most extreme at the North Pole and the South Pole. These places are in total darkness for six months of the year. Their long polar night is followed by a polar day.

Why Polar Nights Occur

A polar night is when the sun does not rise in a particular place in 24 hours or more. A polar night can last for just 24 hours or for many months.

A polar night occurs because Earth tilts as is **orbits** the sun. It tilts at an angle of just over 23.45 degrees. As a result, at different times of the year, sunlight is unable to reach the extreme north and south points of Earth.

▼ During different times of the year, the North and South poles experience polar nights, when no sunlight reaches them.

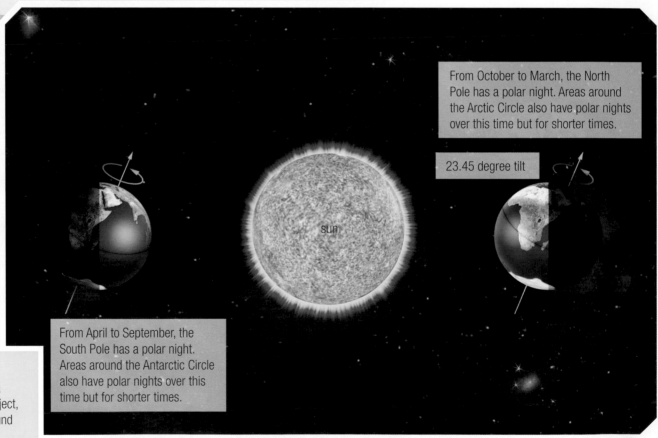

From October to March, the North Pole has a polar night. Areas around the Arctic Circle also have polar nights over this time but for shorter times.

23.45 degree tilt

sun

From April to September, the South Pole has a polar night. Areas around the Antarctic Circle also have polar nights over this time but for shorter times.

Word Watch

orbits moves in a path around an object, such as Earth around the sun

Web Watch ▼

www.wisegeek.com/what-is-a-polar-night.htm

Polar Days

When one pole is experiencing a polar night, the other pole is experiencing the opposite: a polar day. During a polar day, the sun does not set. Like a polar night, a polar day lasts for about six months at the poles.

Polar Auroras

Another polar light **phenomenon** is the polar aurora. A polar aurora is formed when **charged** particles from the sun come in contact with gases in Earth's atmosphere. The collision causes light from the gases to be released into the atmosphere. The light often appears as green ribbons or spiral shapes in the sky.

Polar auroras can only be viewed at the northern and southern areas of Earth because of Earth's magnetic field. Earth is like a giant magnet and the light from an aurora is pulled toward the North or South poles.

▶ In the north, the polar aurora is known as the Northern Lights or *aurora borealis*.

Aurora = Dawn
Aurora borealis is Latin for "northern dawn."
Aurora australis is Latin for "southern dawn."

Word Watch

charged having an electrical charge

phenomenon happening or occurrence

▲ A polar aurora is seen over a base at the South Pole. In the south, the polar aurora is known as *aurora australis*.

Web Watch ▼

www.phy6.org/outreach/edu/aurora.htm

www.antarcticconnection.com/antarctic/weather/aurora.shtm

How Do Periscopes Work?

Periscopes are devices that enable people to see around corners or over high obstacles. Periscopes are most commonly used in submarines, so sailors can see what is happening above the surface of the water.

Reflection

Reflection plays a very important part in how we see things. Most objects do not create their own light. The only way we see them is because light is **reflected** off them and into our eyes. Our eyes take in this light and our brain interprets it.

If you turn all the lights off in your bedroom at night and close the door, you will probably not be able to see your bed. Once a light source enters the room, however, light bounces off your bed and into the **retinas** in your eyes, making the bed visible.

mirror on 45-degree angle

path of light

viewer

mirror on 45-degree angle

▲ A periscope uses a series of mirrors to reflect an image to the viewer.

The Science of Periscopes

Periscopes work by reflecting a light source off two mirrors and into the viewer's eyes. When light enters the top of a periscope, it hits a mirror that is positioned at a 45-degree angle. This top mirror directs the light downward to a second mirror, which is also positioned at a 45-degree angle. This bottom mirror directs the light into the eyes of the viewer.

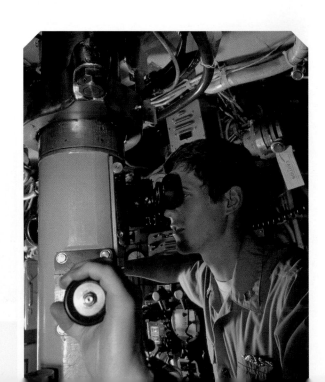

▶ A sailor on a submarine uses a periscope to see above the water's surface.

Make a Periscope

Follow this simple experiment to make your own periscope.

Materials

- ➲ Tall box or carton, such as a tall milk carton
- ➲ Pencil
- ➲ Ruler
- ➲ Scissors
- ➲ Tape
- ➲ 2 small mirrors, preferably square and flat

Steps

1. Using the ruler, draw a line in the top half of the box at a 45-degree angle to the top of the box. Draw another line in the bottom half, at the same angle.

2. Cut along the top line and the bottom line. Make each slit wide enough and long enough to push a mirror through it.

3. Draw and cut slits on the opposite side of the carton, too. Make sure these slits run the same direction as the slits on the other side.

4. Push each mirror through one of the slits, making sure that it pokes out the slit on the other side. Each mirror should fit firmly. The top mirror should have its reflecting side facing down, and the bottom mirror should have its reflecting side facing up.

5. Cut a window in front of the upper mirror. This is so that light can enter and hit the mirror. Turn the carton around. On the other side, cut a window in front of the bottom mirror, too. This one is your viewing window.

6. Look through the viewing window. Move the periscope around, so that you can see as much of your surroundings as possible.

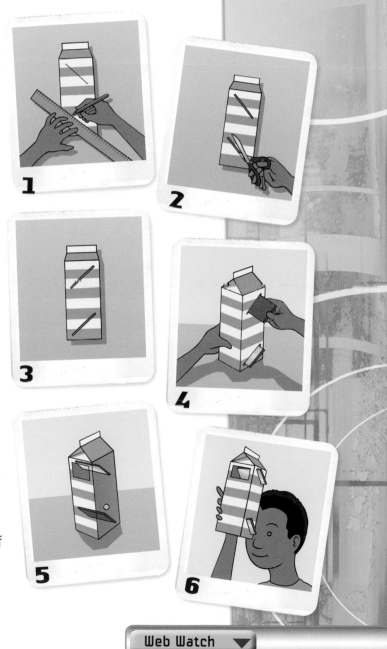

Observation

The image that you see is not a reversed, mirror image. Why is this?

Tricks of Mirrors and Light

Another device that uses mirrors and reflecting light is the kaleidoscope. A kaleidoscope is a toy that reflects colored objects onto mirrors as it is turned.

Web Watch ▼

sub-log.com/eyes_from_the_deep_a_
periscope_history_of_the_us_navy

Why Do Objects in Water Look Closer than They Really Are?

Have you ever reached down to grab something in a swimming pool, only to close your hands around nothing? Objects in water look closer than they really are because of refraction.

What Is Refraction?

Refraction is the bending of light. Refraction occurs because light travels at different speeds through different materials. As a result, when light passes from one material to another (see page 8), its change in speed causes the light wave to bend.

Imagine you are at the beach and running along the sand to get to the water. While you are on the sand, you run fairly smoothly and as fast as you like. Once you hit the water, you are forced to slow down because of the nature of the new material, the water. You cannot travel as fast through the water as you can on the sand. Light works in a similar way.

Looking Into Water

The bending of light is the reason why objects in water look closer than they actually are. The light bends as it enters the water and again when it exits the water. The depth that it appears to be at depends on the angle of the light wave as it enters and exits the water.

Snell's Law

Willebrod Snell (1591–1626) was a Dutch scientist and mathematician who studied the process of refraction and came up with a mathematical law now called Snell's law. Snell's law enables people to work out how much refraction will occur, depending on the angle of the light and the nature of the material that the light passes through.

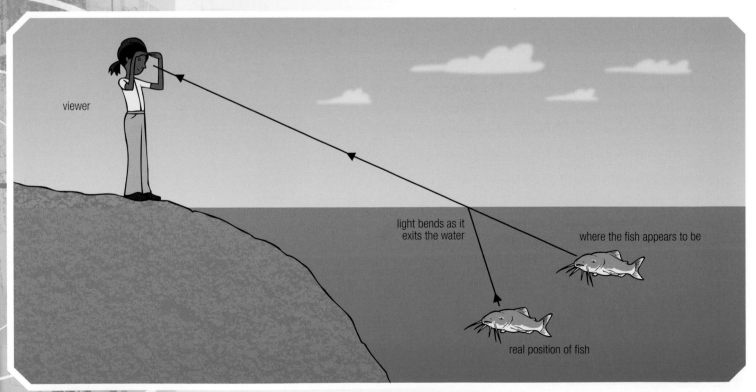

viewer

light bends as it exits the water

where the fish appears to be

real position of fish

▲ The fish appears to be in a different position because of the way the light bends when it exits the water.

Mirages

Refraction does not just make objects in water look closer to the surface than they are, it also creates other **optical illusions**. A **mirage** is caused by refraction. Light travels through warm air at a different speed than through cool air, so people often see distant objects in a different position from where the objects actually are. In some cases, refraction causes a distant surface to appear wet, which is why people in the desert claim to see water in the distance. They walk and walk, searching for the water, but the mirage always appears in the distance, no matter how far they walk.

Try This!

Bend a Pencil

Follow this simple experiment to see how refraction works.

Materials

- Pencil
- Water
- Glass or jar

Steps

1. Fill two-thirds of the glass or jar with water.

2. Place the pencil in the water.

3. Look at the pencil from the side. It appears to be broken, almost as if there are two pencils, one above the water and the other below the water.

4. Look at the pencil from above. The pencil appears to bend.

Word Watch

mirage optical illusion caused by light passing through air of differing temperatures

optical illusions things that the eye sees but that are not real

Web Watch ▼

www.good-science-fair-projects.com/refraction-8.html

Why Does the Sound of a Car Change as It Passes By?

Try This!

Understanding Frequency

To understand how the frequency of sound waves changes because an object moves, try the following experiment. The oranges represent sound waves.

1. Stand still while someone in front of you throws oranges at you at five-second intervals. The oranges will reach you at five-second intervals.

2. Get the person throwing oranges to move toward you, still throwing the oranges at five-second intervals. The oranges will reach you at a faster and faster pace, or frequency.

3. Get the person to walk farther and farther away from you. The oranges will take longer and longer to reach you.

Word Watch

frequency number of times something occurs in a given time period

stationary still or motionless

pitch level or tone of a sound

The sound of a car changes as it gets closer and changes again as the car moves farther away from you. This has to do with the changing **frequency** of the sound waves that you receive. This is called the Doppler effect.

The Doppler Effect

The change in sound produced by a moving object is known as the Doppler effect. When a moving object produces sound, its movement causes the sound waves in front of it to squash together, while the sound waves behind it spread out. This means that someone standing **stationary** will receive sound waves at a more rapid rate as the object gets closer. The closer together or more compressed the sound waves are, the higher the **pitch** of the sound.

▲ The sound that the children hear changes as the car passes by.

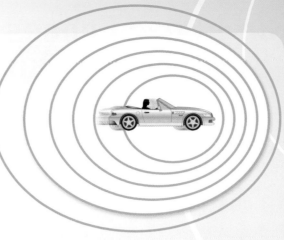

▲ When a stationary object, such as a radio, produces sound, the sound waves it sends out reach you at the same frequency.

▲ When a moving object, such as a car, produces sound, the sound waves in front of it reach you at an increasing frequency and the sound waves behind it reach you at a decreasing frequency.

Christian Doppler

Christian Doppler (1803–1853) was an Austrian mathematician and scientist. He conducted experiments after observing that sound from moving objects changed as the objects passed him. His experiments proved his **observations** correct and this effect became known as the Doppler effect.

Try This!

Test the Doppler Effect

Follow this simple experiment to illustrate how the Doppler effect works. You do not have to use a whistle. A horn, siren, or bell should produce the same effect.

Materials

↻ Friend ↻ Bicycle ↻ Whistle

Steps

1. Get your friend to blow the whistle, while he or she sits on a bike about 100 feet (30 m) away. Because your friend is not moving, the sound waves spread out evenly in all directions.

2. Get your friend to ride toward you as fast as he or she can, while continually blowing on the whistle. You should hear the pitch of the whistle get a little higher as they approach.

3. Your friend should continue riding and blowing the whistle until he or she has passed you by about 30 feet (10 m). As your friend passes and starts to cycle away from you, the pitch of the whistle should sound a little lower.

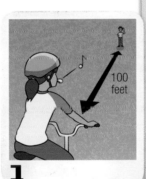

1

2

3

Word Watch

observations
information that is gained by watching something carefully

Measuring Speed Using the Doppler Effect

The Doppler effect occurs with all types of waves. Police radar devices use radio waves to measure the speed of cars. The radar device sends out radio waves at a particular frequency and measures the frequency of the waves that bounce back off the car.

Web Watch ▼

www.earthsky.org/kids/46142/the-doppler-effect

Why Can I Hear Echoes in Some Places But Not in Others?

Echoes occur when sound waves are **reflected** off a surface. Some surfaces produce great echoes. Other surfaces **absorb** sound waves and do not produce echoes at all.

Creating an Echo

The properties of nearby surfaces determine the **clarity** of an echo and whether an echo is given out or not. The harder, smoother, and flatter a surface, the clearer the echo. The distance between the surface and the origin of the sound also plays a part. The origin of the sound cannot be too close to the surface. If sound waves hit a surface within 0.1 seconds—about 56 feet (17 m)—of the sound being produced, there is no echo.

Word Watch

absorb soak up and reduce the effect of

clarity clearness

reflected returned or bounced back

▲ Sound waves bounce easily off a hard, flat surface, such as a wall. If the origin of the sound is close to the wall, there is no echo. Instead, the original sound seems to be extended. This is known as reverberation.

▲ When sound waves hit a soft surface, such as a cushion, most of the sound is absorbed and not reflected.

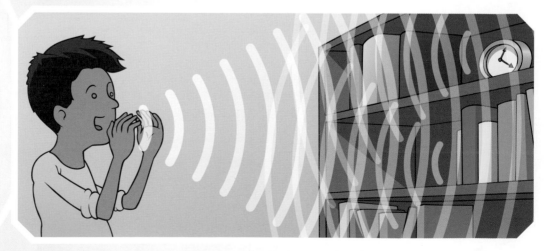

▲ Surfaces that have both hard and soft properties, such as a bookshelf, reflect some of the sound waves and absorb some of the sound waves.

Inside a Concert Hall

Concert halls are specially designed to absorb some sounds and reflect other sounds. Curved objects are hung around the hall, facing different directions, to reflect some sound waves. Soft objects are used to absorb sound so that echoes do not ruin the experience of the audience. The aim is that the orchestra sounds the same no matter where an audience member sits.

▶ The shape and textures used in a concert hall are chosen to absorb and reflect sounds from different parts of the hall.

Try This! Create Echoes

This experiment shows how the angle that sound waves bounce off surfaces affects the volume of an echo.

Materials

- Wall
- 2 tubes
- Clock that ticks

Steps

1. Place the clock on the floor. Put an end of one of the tubes next to the clock and put the other end against the wall at a 45-degree angle.

2. Put an end of the other tube against the wall to catch the echoes. Holding it at a 45-degree angle, place your ear over the other end of the tube. You should hear the echo of the ticking clock.

3. Change the angle of the tube that you are listening through. Observe how the volume and clarity of the echo changes as the angle changes.

Web Watch ▼

www.scientificamerican.com/article.cfm?id=how-do-bats-echolocate-an

Why Can Dogs Hear Sounds that Humans Cannot Hear?

Dogs can hear sounds that humans cannot hear. So can dolphins, rats, bats, and cats! This is because these animals have a greater **frequency** range than humans.

Frequency Range of Dogs

Dogs can hear a greater frequency range than humans. They have developed this **characteristic** over millions of years, relying on good hearing to source food and protect themselves from **predators**.

▲ A dog whistle gives out a sound that is too high for humans to hear, but which dogs can hear.

Animal	Average Hearing Range (Hertz)
Tuna	50–1,100
Chicken	125–2,000
Goldfish	20–3,000
Bullfrog	100–3,000
Catfish	50–4,000
Tree frog	50–4,000
Canary	250–8,000
Elephant	16–12,000
Owl	200–12,000
Human	64–23,000
Sheep	100–30,000
Horse	55–33,500
Cow	23–35,000
Raccoon	100–40,000
Rabbit	360–42,000
Dog	67–45,000
Hedgehog	250–45,000
Guinea pig	54–50,000
Gerbil	100–60,000
Cat	45–64,000
Opossum	500–64,000
Rat	200–76,000
Mouse	1,000–91,000
Bat	2,000–110,000
Beluga whale	1,000–123,000
Porpoise and dolphin	75–150,000

Source: www.lsu.edu/deafness/HearingRange.html

Frequency is the number of vibrations, or sound waves, that a sound produces each second. The more vibrations there are, the higher the sound. The fewer vibrations, the deeper the sound.

Frequency is measured in units called hertz (Hz). If a sound has a frequency of 3,000 Hz, it produces 3,000 vibrations each second. Most humans can hear sounds between 64 and 23,000 Hz. Dogs can hear sounds between 67 and 45,000 Hz. There are many sounds that dogs can hear that are too high for a human to hear. There are also a few very low sounds that humans can hear but dogs cannot.

Frequency Ranges of Other Animals

Different animals can hear different frequency ranges. The table (left) is arranged in order of the least highest frequencies to the highest frequencies.

Dolphins and Porpoises

Dolphins and porpoises are able to hear sounds up to 170,000 Hz in frequency and as low as 7 Hz. One reason that they have such a wide range of hearing is that it is extremely hard to see underwater because of the lack of light. Hearing is an essential part of their survival.

▶ Dolphins communicate using very high-pitched sounds that are well outside the hearing range of other animals.

Try This! Create Different Frequencies

This experiment shows how different frequencies produce different sounds.

Materials

- 8 clean glasses
- Water
- Metal teaspoon

Steps

1. Place the glasses next to each other on a table.

2. Fill the first glass one-eighth full with water.

3. Fill the second glass one-quarter full with water.

4. Continue the process, filling each glass with a little bit more than the one before it.

5. Fill the last glass almost to its brim.

6. Tap the glasses above the water line with the spoon, one at a time. Listen closely to the sound each one makes.

Observation

The tapping of the teaspoon causes the glasses to vibrate. The water slows down the vibrations. The less water and the more air there is in a glass, the greater the frequency and the higher the sound.

1

2

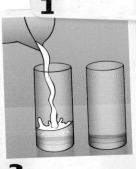
4

6

Large Ears for High Frequencies

Land animals that are able to hear high frequency sounds generally have large ears compared to their body size. Large ears help direct the sound into the ear. Mice, dogs, and cats are examples of land animals with relatively large ears compared to their body sizes.

Decreasing Range

A human's ability to hear high frequency sounds decreases with age. By the time a person reaches about 45 years old, he or she may not be able to hear sounds higher than 15,000 Hz.

Can a High Note From an Opera Singer Really Cause a Glass to Shatter?

Many movies, cartoons, and television programs have featured an opera singer shattering a glass by singing and holding a very high note. In reality, it is extremely difficult to do this.

Shattering a Glass

Under laboratory conditions, scientists can shatter a glass using sound. Three critical factors must be in place:

- ⮞ the right glass
- ⮞ the right note
- ⮞ the right volume

The Right Glass

The glass should be a wine glass and it should be as thin as possible. Most importantly, the glass must have flaws in it. Most glasses have tiny cracks in them that cannot be seen, except under a microscope. The cheaper the glass, the greater the chance it has the necessary flaws.

The Right Note

The best chance of shattering a glass is to identify the natural **resonant frequency** of the glass and use that sound. The natural resonant frequency is the speed at which a glass will vibrate when hit by an object or by sound waves. The natural resonant frequency can be heard by tapping the glass with a metal spoon. A scientist would try to **replicate** this sound.

The Right Volume

Once the sound waves have set the glass vibrating, the glass needs to be bombarded by more and more sound waves. If the glass vibrates for long enough, it will shatter. This requires a great deal of volume. An **amplifier** can be used to increase the volume of the sound to at least 100 **decibels**.

Word Watch

amplifier electronic device that increases the volume of a sound

decibels unit by which the volume of sound is measured

frequency number of times something occurs in a given time period

replicate copy

resonant echoing vibration

▲ Some opera singers can sing and hold very high notes.

Measuring the Volume of Sound

The volume of sound is measured in decibels (dB). Decibels actually measure a sound's energy **intensity** but this is equivalent to the amount of noise it makes.

The quietest sounds that the human ear can hear are about 10 dB. Sounds of 90 dB and higher can cause damage to hearing.

► A military jet taking off is about 130 dB.

► An underground train is about 90 dB.

► Normal conversation is about 60 dB.

► The ticking of a watch is about 20 dB.

140 dB
130 dB
120 dB
110 dB
100 dB
90 dB
80 dB
70 dB
60 dB
50 dB
40 dB
30 dB
20 dB
10 dB
0 dB

◄ A very loud rock concert measures about 100 dB.

◄ Traffic on a busy street is about 70 dB.

◄ A quiet classroom at exam time is about 40 dB.

◄ The rustling of leaves in the wind is equal to about 10 dB.

Bels and Decibels

The decibel was named after Alexander Graham Bell (1847–1922), who was a scientist and the inventor of the telephone. Bell Laboratories came up with a unit of measurement for sound, which they called the bel. It was too large to measure everyday sounds, so they came up with a smaller version, called the decibel.

Word Watch

intensity strength

29

How Do Hearing Aids Work?

Hearing aids **amplify** sound so that people with hearing problems are able to hear sounds they could not otherwise hear. Some hearing aids are worn in the ear, while others are worn behind the ear.

How We Hear

The ear is the organ used for hearing. It allows us to hear sounds and make sense of sound waves.

The outer ear is known as the pinna or auricle. Its shape helps gather sound waves from the surrounding environment and send them down the ear canal.

Sound waves enter the middle ear and cause the eardrum to vibrate. These vibrations travel to three tiny bones, called the malleus, incus, and stapes. Together, these bones are known as the ossicles. The ossicles send the vibrations to the inner ear.

In the inner ear is a shell-shaped organ, called the cochlea. The cochlea is filled with liquid and tiny hairs. When the vibrations reach the cochlea, nerves on the ends of the hairs **transmit** the vibrations as messages to the brain, where the messages are processed and identified as sounds.

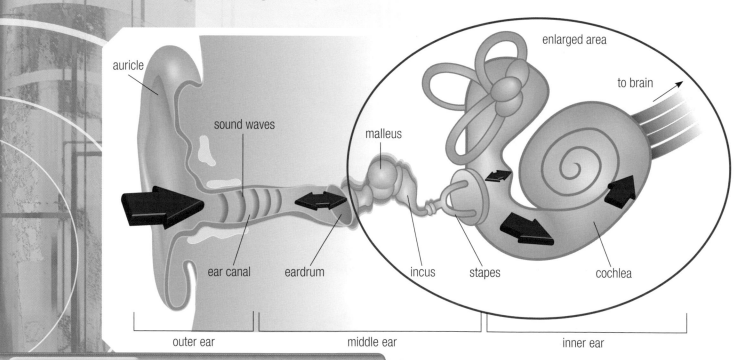

auricle

sound waves

enlarged area

to brain

malleus

ear canal   eardrum   incus   stapes   cochlea

outer ear   middle ear   inner ear

▲ The human ear is made up of the outer, middle, and inner ears.

The Hearing Aid

Some people cannot hear due to hearing loss or deafness. They can use hearing aids to help them hear. The key parts of a hearing aid are:

- a microphone that picks up sounds and changes them into electrical signals
- an amplifier that makes the sound louder
- a speaker or receiver that changes the electrical signals back into sounds
- a battery that keeps the electrical circuits operating
- an ear hook that keeps the hearing aid in place
- an ear mold that directs the sound to the ear canal

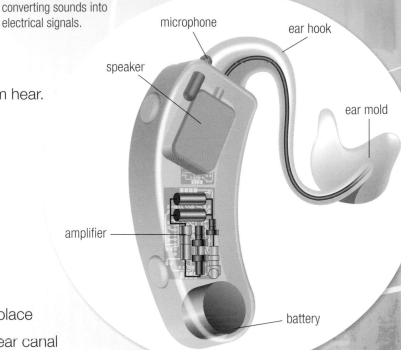

▶ Hearing aids work by converting sounds into electrical signals.

microphone

ear hook

speaker

ear mold

amplifier

battery

Try This!

Make an Ear Trumpet

Make an ear trumpet and see how it amplifies sound.

Materials

- 3 or 4 sheets of paper—about 9 inches x 11 inches (22 cm x 28 cm)
- Roll of tape
- Pair of scissors
- Sound source, such as a radio

Instructions

1. Roll one piece of paper into a cone, so the opening is about 2 inches (5 cm) wide.

2. Tape the edges of the paper so that it does not come apart.

3. Cut out a handle (this is optional).

4. Listen to the sound source without the cone. Then, listen to the sound source again, with the cone to your ear. Note the difference.

5. Tape two pieces of paper together and make a larger cone.

6. Listen to the sound source again, first without the large cone and then with the large cone. Note the difference.

7. Cut the first cone in half to make it smaller. Listen to the sound source again. Is there a difference to the first time you used it?

Index